MOCKTAILS

NONALCOHOLIC COCKTAILS WITH TASTE AND STYLE

Caroline Hwang

Photography by Beatriz da Costa

weldon**owen**

MOCKTAILS

NON-ALCOHOLIC COCKTAILS WITH TASTE AND STYLE

Caroline Hwang

Photography by Beatriz da Costa

MARABOUT

CONTENTS

INTRODUCTION

When you host a gathering, you naturally want to be thoughtful and consider your guests' needs and dietary restrictions. While you may not be able to cater to everyone who has a gluten-free, sugar-free, or dairy-free diet, you can easily have both alcoholic and nonalcoholic beverages available—and the nonalcoholic drinks don't have to be water or fizzy drinks. Alcohol-free beverages can be fun, delicious, inventive, and just as well thought out as the other drinks you've decided to have on your menu.

Most of the recipes in this book yield one serving, but they can be easily multiplied to serve more—just be careful as to how much liquid you shake in a cocktail shaker as it can only hold so much. All the drinks made in a pitcher yield four to six servings.

Many drinks in this book are made in a cocktail shaker, because mocktail making follows the same philosophy as cocktail making: when there is citrus, egg white, or cream, they should be shaken, as you want them to be fully combined, full of air bubbles, and ice-cold. Of course, there are a few exceptions, but that is the general rule of thumb. You will also want to double strain instead of simply using a cocktail strainer to remove the excess citrus bits from your drink. You want your drink to be as aesthetically pleasing as it is pleasant to your taste buds. After all, we do eat—and drink—with our eyes first.

Making or creating a mocktail isn't difficult—sometimes all it takes is an infused simple syrup, citrus juice, and soda water. In this book, you will find creative and different takes on that simple foundation. Soon enough, you will be inventing mocktail recipes on your own. Cheers!

EQUIPMENT

*Here are the essential tools that will help you make
the perfect mocktail for any occasion.*

1.

2.

3.

4.

1. COCKTAIL SHAKER
Ideal for mixing drinks, especially shaken drinks, cocktail shakers fully combine all the flavors together.

2. HAWTHORNE STRAINER
Indispensable for straining out chunks of ice and other large pieces.

3. FINE-MESH STRAINER
Necessary for straining out tiny pieces of ice that will dilute your drink further, as well as for keeping your drink nice and clean looking.

4. JIGGER
For measuring small amounts of liquid.

5.

6.

7.

8.

5. STIR SPOON
A long bar spoon is preferable, but you could use any spoon to mix these mocktails.

6. BLENDER
Blenders are perfect for making piña coladas and other slushy drinks.

7. PINT GLASS
A pint glass is useful for stirring drinks before straining them into your final glassware.

8. CITRUS JUICER
Citrus is required for many of these mocktails; a juicer will make life easier for you.

MOCKTAIL NECESSITIES

A well-stocked bar is essential for making mocktails, so be sure to have these items on hand and you will be well on the way to making delicious drinks.

THE BASE: *Sodas, tonic water, fruit juices, and milks such as rice and coconut milk*

SOME SWEETNESS: *Including maple syrup and honey, granulated and brown sugar, and pomegranate molasses*

FRUITS & VEGETABLES, FRESH & DRIED: *Such as fresh berries, oranges, apples, peaches, bananas, celery, cucumber, dried persimmon, and mango*

FRESH HERBS & FLOWERS:
Such as thyme, sage, basil, mint, and lavender

ACIDS FOR JUICE, ZEST & PEEL: *Such as lemons, limes, oranges, and grapefruit*

DRIED SPICES & FLOWERS: *Such as cinnamon, hibiscus flowers, chile, and matcha (green tea) powder*

TEAS & COFFEE:
Such as Lapsang Souchong and chai

GARNISH:
Including Morello cherries, fresh fruit, and herbs

ICE:
And plenty of it!

SIMPLE SYRUP

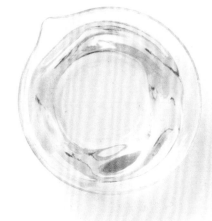

makes 5 fl oz (about ½ cup)

½ cup sugar
4 fl oz (½ cup) water

Heat sugar and water and stir
to dissolve sugar. Let cool.

HERB-Y BLEND

makes 5 fl oz (about ½ cup)

½ cup sugar
4 fl oz (½ cup) water
handful each of mint, basil, lemon verbena

Heat sugar and water and stir to dissolve
sugar. Remove from heat and let cool.
Blanch herbs for 15 seconds. Pick leaves
and blend (in a blender) with sugar syrup.

APPLE & GINGER

makes 5 fl oz (about ½ cup)

½ cup sugar
4 fl oz (½ cup) water
6 pieces of apple peels
1½-inch piece of ginger, peeled and chopped

Heat sugar and water in a pan, stirring to dissolve sugar. Add apple peel and ginger and simmer for 30 minutes, then strain and let cool.

ALLSPICE

makes 5 fl oz (about ½ cup)

½ cup sugar
4 fl oz (½ cup) water
2 tablespoons. crushed allspice

Heat sugar and water and stir to dissolve sugar. Add allspice and simmer for 10 minutes. Remove from heat and let steep for 30 minutes. Strain through a double layer of cheesecloth.

LEMON

makes 7 fl oz (⅞ cup)

1 cup superfine sugar
zest of 6 lemons
2 fl oz (¼ cup) hot water

Place sugar and zest in a resealable plastic bag and massage together. Let rest for 1 hour. Add hot water to dissolve any remaining sugar. Strain. Chill for up to 2 weeks.

MEYER LEMON

makes 7 fl oz (⅞ cup)

1 cup superfine sugar
zest of 6 Meyer lemons
2 fl oz (¼ cup) hot water

Place zest and sugar in a resealable plastic bag and massage together. Let rest for 1 hour. Add hot water to dissolve any remaining sugar. Strain. Chill for up to 2 weeks.

GRAPEFRUIT

makes 7 fl oz (⅞ cup)

1 cup superfine sugar
zest of 4 grapefruit
2 fl oz (¼ cup) hot water

Place sugar and zest in a resealable plastic bag and massage together. Let rest for 1 hour. Add hot water to dissolve any remaining sugar. Strain. Chill for up to 2 weeks.

KAFFIR LIME & ROSEMARY

makes 7 fl oz (⅞ cup)

1 cup superfine sugar
zest of 8 kaffir limes
leaves of 4 rosemary sprigs, chopped
2 fl oz (¼ cup) hot water

Place sugar, zest, and rosemary in a bowl and massage together. Place in a resealable plastic bag and let rest for 1 hour. Add hot water to dissolve any remaining sugar. Strain. Chill for up to 2 weeks.

STRAWBERRY & RHUBARB

makes 20 fl oz (2½ cups)

½ lb strawberries, hulled and halved
4 rhubarb stalks, chopped
1¼ cups granulated sugar
1 teaspoon salt
1 cup champagne vinegar

Place all ingredients in a small pan over medium-high heat and let rhubarb cook down for about 10 minutes. Remove from heat and strain through two layers of cheesecloth. Store in refrigerator.

PLUM & CINNAMON

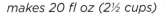

makes 20 fl oz (2½ cups)

3 small plums, quartered and stoned
3 cinnamon sticks
1⅛ cups granulated sugar
4 fl oz (½ cup) apple cider vinegar

Gently mix everything, except vinegar, in a bowl. Cover and leave at room temperature, stirring every 2 hours, for 24 hours.
Stir in vinegar. Leave for 1 day at room temperature. Strain through two layers of cheesecloth. Store in refrigerator.

CRANBERRY & SAGE

makes 20 fl oz (2½ cups)

2¼ cups cranberries
½ cup sugar
4 fl oz (½ cup) water
4 sage leaves
4 fl oz (½ cup) apple cider vinegar

Simmer cranberries, sugar, and water gently until cranberries pop. Add sage, then let cool and strain, pressing down on cranberries to extract liquid. Stir in vinegar to liquid. Store in refrigerator.

APRICOT

Gently mix everything, except vinegar, in a bowl. Cover and leave at room temperature, stirring every 2 hours, for 24 hours. Stir in vinegar. Leave for 1 day at room temperature. Strain through muslin. Store in refrigerator.

makes 20 fl oz (2½ cups)

4 small apricots, quartered and pitted
1¼ cups granulated sugar
4 fl oz (½ cup) coconut vinegar

SPICED PERSIMMON

varies depending on fruit size

2 very ripe persimmons, peeled and chopped
1 teaspoon ground cinnamon
¼ teaspoon ground cloves
1 teaspoon maple syrup

Place all ingredients in a blender and purée. Chill for 7–10 days.

ROASTED PEAR

varies depending on fruit size

2 pears, peeled and roughly chopped
1 tablespoon honey
1 vanilla pod, split lengthwise and seeds
   scraped out

Preheat oven to 375°F. Toss ingredients together on a baking sheet, cover with foil, and roast for 20–30 minutes until soft. Let pears cool then purée in a blender, adding a little water if too thick. Chill for 7–10 days.

WINTER SQUASH

varies depending on squash size

1 winter squash (such as butternut, pumpkin, acorn, kabocha), peeled, seeded and sliced into 2-inch slices

⅔ cup brown sugar

Preheat oven to 375°F. Toss ingredients together on a baking sheet, cover with foil, and roast for 20–30 minutes until soft. Let squash cool, then purée in a blender, adding water if too thick. Chill for 7–10 days.

SMOKED PINEAPPLE

varies depending on fruit size

1 lb pineapple, peeled and sliced lengthwise
2 tablespoons brown sugar
4 fl oz (½ cup) water

Preheat grill. Place pineapple slices on a baking sheet in a single layer. Grill until beginning to char to a medium golden brown. Add brown sugar and caramelize and char under grill. Cool, then purée, adding water as needed. Chill for 7–10 days.

CHILE BLACK SALT

makes about ⅓ cup

1 tablespoon cayenne pepper
⅓ cup black salt

Mix ingredients together and
store in an airtight jar.

CELERY PINK SALT

makes about ⅓ cup

3 teaspoons celery seed
⅓ cup pink himalayan salt

Mix ingredients together and
store in an airtight jar.

TOGARASHI SALT

makes about ⅓ cup

2 tablespoons togarashi
⅓ cup sea salt

Mix ingredients together and store
in an airtight jar.

WILD FENNEL SUGAR

makes about ⅓ cup

3 teaspoons fennel pollen
⅓ cup granulated sugar

Mix ingredients together and store
in an airtight jar.

4 fl oz (½ cup) soda water

1 fl oz (⅛ cup) lemon juice

¼ teaspoon matcha
(green tea) powder

½ oz Simple Syrup (see page 12)

lemon peel, for garnish

MATCHA MAKER

Preparation: 5 minutes
Serve in a tall glass

Mix matcha powder and syrup together in a shaker. Add lemon juice
and ice, then shake. Pour soda water into shaker and stir until combined.
Strain into a tall glass filled with fresh ice. Garnish with lemon peel.

water, to top

1 fl oz (⅛ cup) Simple Syrup
(see page 12)

2 fl oz (¼ cup) lemon juice

4 strawberries, hulled and quartered,
plus more for garnish

3 thyme sprigs, plus more for garnish

STRAWBERRY-THYME COOLER

Preparation: 5 minutes
Serve in a tall glass

Muddle strawberries and thyme in a cocktail shaker. Add remaining
ingredients, except for the water, and shake vigorously.
Double strain into a chilled tall glass filled with ice and
top with water. Garnish with a strawberry and thyme sprig.

handful of lychees, peeled and pitted, plus more for garnish

1 fl oz (⅛ cup) Simple Syrup (see page 12)

12 fl oz (1½ cups) soda water

12 fl oz (1½ cups) lychee juice

2 fl oz (¼ cup) lemon juice

6 mint leaves, plus more for garnish

LYCHEE-TINI

Preparation: 5 minutes
Serve in a pitcher and rocks glasses

Purée fruit, lychee juice, and mint in a blender.
Strain and add lemon juice and syrup. When ready to serve,
pour into a 3½-cup pitcher, top with soda water, and stir.
Serve over ice, garnished with mint sprigs and lychees.

soda water, to top

¼ cup pineapple, peeled and
roughly chopped

¼ cup Smoked
Pineapple Purée
(see page 19)

3 mint sprigs,
plus more for garnish

pineapple wedge,
for garnish

PINEAPPLE MINT SPRITZ

Preparation: 5 minutes
Serve in a Collins glass

Muddle pineapple and mint evenly in a Collins glass.
Add ice and purée to glass, then top with soda water. Stir.
Serve, garnished with a pineapple wedge and mint.

1½ fl oz (3 tablespoons)
Apricot Shrub (see page 17)

2 fl oz (¼ cup) apricot juice

sparkling apple juice, to top

APRICOT BELLINI

Preparation: 5 minutes
Serve in a Champagne glass

Combine Apricot Shrub and apricot juice in a cocktail shaker and stir until combined. Pour into a Champagne glass, top with apple juice and stir.

soda water, to top

1 lime wedge

handful of blueberries,
plus more for garnish

1 fl oz (⅛ cup) cardamom simple
syrup (Heat 2 tablespoons ground
cardamom, ¾ cup sugar, and ¾ cup water
together until dissolved. Let cool.)

BLUEBERRY CARDAMOM SMASH

Preparation: 10 minutes
Serve in a rocks glass

Muddle blueberries and lime wedge in a rocks glass,
add syrup, and stir well. Add ice and top with soda water.
Garnish with remaining blueberries.

16 fl oz (2 cups) mixed berry juice

8 fl oz (1 cup) sparkling lemonade

2 fl oz (¼ cup) lemon verbena
simple syrup (Heat a handful of lemon
verbena leaves, ¾ cup sugar, and ¾ cup
water together until dissolved. Let cool.)

2 fl oz (¼ cup) lime juice

lemon slices and berries,
for garnish

BERRY PUNCH

Preparation: 10 minutes
Serve in a pitcher and tall glasses

Stir all the ingredients together in a large pitcher. Add ice,
lemon slices, and berries to tall glasses and serve.

4 fl oz (½ cup) jasmine tea
(strongly brewed), chilled

1½ fl oz (3 tablespoons) condensed milk

1½ fl oz (3 tablespoons)
coconut milk

¾ fl oz (1½ tablespoons) cinnamon simple
syrup (Heat 3 cinnamon sticks, ¾ cup sugar,
and ¾ cup water together until dissolved. Remove
from heat and let steep for 30 minutes. Strain.)

JASMINE COCONUT MILK TEA

Preparation: 10 minutes
Serve in a tall or Collins glass

Combine all the ingredients in a cocktail shaker and shake vigorously.
Strain into a tall or Collins glass filled with crushed ice.

2 fl oz (¼ cup) sumac tea, chilled

1 egg white

¾ fl oz (1½ tablespoons) Herb-y Blend
Syrup (see page 12)

1 fl oz (2 tablespoons)
pomegranate juice

SUMAC SOUR

Preparation: 5 minutes
Serve in a Champagne glass

Combine all the ingredients in a cocktail shaker and dry shake until
the egg white is emulsified, about 20–30 seconds. Add ice and
shake again until chilled. Strain evenly into 2 glasses.

soda water, to top

2 fl oz (¼ cup) double cream

2 fl oz (¼ cup) lemon juice

1 tablespoon
cherry jelly

1 fl oz (2 tablespoons) Cardamom
Simple Syrup (see page 32)

whipped cream and cherry,
for garnish

CHERRY CARDAMOM FIZZ

Preparation: 10 minutes
Serve in a tall or Collins glass

Combine all the ingredients, except for the soda water,
in a cocktail shaker with ice and shake until chilled. Strain into
a tall or Collins glass filled with fresh ice and top with soda
water. Garnish with whipped cream and a cherry.

ginger beer, to top

berries and lime slices, for garnish

1 fl oz (2 tablespoons) lime juice

2 fl oz (¼ cup) mixed berry juice

BERRY MOSCOW MULE

Preparation: 5 minutes
Serve in a rocks glass or copper mug

Combine berry and lime juices in a glass or mug filled with ice and stir.
Top with ginger beer and garnish with berries and limes.

4 fl oz (½ cup) water

1½ fl oz (3 tablespoons)
coconut milk

1 Medjool date, pitted

2½ fl oz (⅓ cup) rice milk

¾ fl oz (1½ tablespoons)
Simple Syrup (see page 12)

1¾ tablespoons toasted
black sesame seeds,
plus more for garnish

BLACK SESAME MILK

Preparation: 10 minutes
Serve in a tall glass

Simmer sesame seeds, date, and water gently in a small pan.
Transfer mixture to a blender and blend until puréed. Strain and let cool.
Combine black sesame seed mixture with remaining ingredients in a
cocktail shaker with ice and shake until chilled. Strain into a tall glass
filled with fresh ice and garnish with remaining sesame seeds.

12 fl oz (1½ cups) tomato juice

juice of 1 lime

¼ cup finely
grated ginger

1 teaspoon Sriracha sauce
(or more depending on how
much spiciness you like)

2 fl oz (¼ cup)
Worcestershire sauce

½ cup kimchee and juices

1½ tablespoons rice
wine vinegar

BLOODY DO-MAH-DO

Preparation: 5 minutes
Serve in a pitcher and rocks glasses

Combine all the ingredients in a large pitcher and stir well.
Pour into rocks glasses filled with ice and serve.

soda water, to top

4 fl oz (½ cup) rice milk

½ teaspoon cayenne pepper

1 cinnamon stick

1 tablespoon
brown sugar

⅓ cup mexican chocolate or good-
quality dark chocolate, shaved

ground cinnamon,
for garnish

MEXICAN CHOCOLATE FIZZ

Preparation: 5 minutes
Serve in a rocks glass

Place chocolate, milk, cayenne, and cinnamon stick in a small pan and
bring to a low simmer for 5 minutes, stirring frequently. Add sugar
and stir until dissolved. Let cool, then place cooled mixture and ice in
a cocktail shaker and shake. Pour into a rocks glass filled with fresh ice
and top with soda water. Garnish with ground cinnamon.

2 fl oz (¼ cup) lime juice

1 fl oz (2 tablespoons) soda water

1 fl oz (2 tablespoons) Kaffir Lime & Rosemary
Oleo Saccharum (see page 15)

2 kaffir lime leaves, plus more for garnish

THAI DAIQUIRI

Preparation: 5 minutes
Serve in a Coupe glass

Muddle kaffir lime leaves in a pint glass, add remaining
ingredients and ice. Gently stir together, then strain
into a Coupe glass. Garnish with a lime leaf.

soda water, to top

3 fl oz (6 tablespoons)
white grape juice

½ fl oz (1 tablespoon)
grenadine

¾ fl oz (1½ tablespoons) lavender
simple syrup (Heat ¾ cup sugar, ¾ cup water,
and 1 tablespoon dried lavender together until
sugar has dissolved. Let cool and strain.)

lavender sprig, for garnish

LAVENDER BUBBLY

Preparation: 5 minutes
Serve in a Champagne glass

Mix all the ingredients, except for the soda water and lavender sprig,
together in a Champagne glass. Top with soda water and
gently stir to incorporate. Garnish with lavender.

1 tablespoon cherry jelly

2 fl oz (¼ cup) lime juice

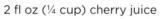

2 fl oz (¼ cup) cherry juice

1 fl oz (2 tablespoons)
aloe vera juice

1 maraschino cherry, for garnish

CHERRY VERA

Preparation: 5 minutes
Serve in a stemmed glass

Place all the ingredients, except for the maraschino cherry,
in a cocktail shaker filled with ice. Shake vigorously, then
double strain into a chilled glass. Garnish with the maraschino cherry.

soda water, to top

4 fl oz (½ cup) raspberry juice

1 fl oz (2 tablespoons)
elderflower syrup

2 fl oz (¼ cup) white grape juice

1 raspberry, for garnish

RASPBERRY FAUX CHAMPAGNE

Preparation: 6 minutes
Serve in a Champagne glass

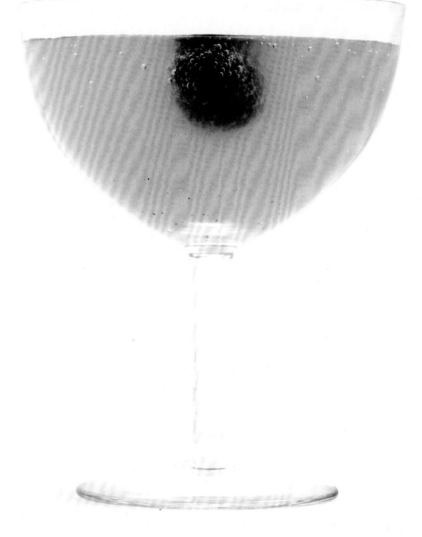

Combine all the ingredients, except for the raspberry, in a mixing
glass and stir with ice until chilled. Strain into a Champagne glass,
top with soda water, and garnish with a raspberry.

lemon-lime soda, to top

2 fl oz (¼ cup) lime juice

1 teaspoon
red pepper flakes

¼ lb watermelon,
seeded and diced

1 teaspoon grated lime zest

Chile Black Salt
(see page 20), for rim

STREET WATERMELON JUICE

Preparation: 10 minutes
Serve in a tall glass

Combine all the ingredients, except for the soda and salt, in a blender
with ½ cup ice. Salt rim of a tall glass with Chile Black Salt, then pour
blended drink into glass and top with soda.

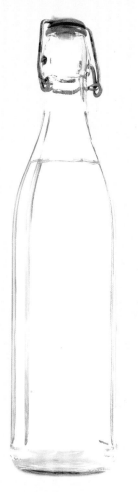

4 cups water

lemon slices,
for garnish (optional)

½ cup granulated sugar

1 cup lemon juice

LEMONADE

Preparation: 5 minutes
Serve in a large pitcher with tall glasses

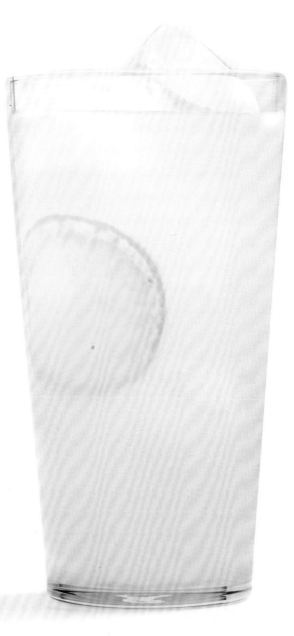

Combine sugar and lemon juice in a large pitcher and stir until sugar is dissolved.
Add water and serve over ice, garnished with lemon slices if you like.

2 fl oz (¼ cup) coconut water

2 fl oz (¼ cup) lime juice

2 fl oz (¼ cup) hot water

1 fl oz (2 tablespoons)
Simple Syrup
(see page 12)

pinch of hibiscus flowers,
plus lime slices and hibiscus
flowers, for garnish

¼ cup crushed ice

HIBISCUS LIME SLUSH

Preparation: 5 minutes,
plus 30 minutes steeping
Serve in a tall glass

Combine hibiscus flowers and hot water in a heatproof pitcher and steep for
30 minutes, or until it cools to room temperature. Strain, then combine with
lime juice, coconut water, syrup, and ¼ cup ice in a blender and blend until slushy.
Serve in a tall glass with a straw and garnished with a lime slice and hibiscus flowers.

tonic water, to top

2 fl oz (¼ cup) lime juice

1 fl oz (2 tablespoons)
elderflower syrup

2 fl oz (¼ cup) water

3 cucumber slices

thin cucumber strip,
for garnish

CUCUMBER ELDERFLOWER FIZZ

Preparation: 5 minutes
Serve in a rocks glass

Muddle cucumber slices in a cocktail shaker, add syrup, lime juice, water,
and ice and shake. Double strain into a rocks glass filled with fresh ice.
Top with tonic water and garnish with a cucumber strip.

3 fl oz (6 tablespoons)
pineapple juice

pineapple wedge, maraschino cherry,
and mint sprig, for garnish

⅔ cup crushed ice

4 fl oz (½ cup) cream of coconut

PIÑA COLADA

Preparation: 5 minutes
Serve in a tall glass

Combine pineapple juice, ice, and cream of coconut in a blender
and blend until smooth. Pour into a tall glass and garnish with
a pineapple wedge, cherry, and mint.

7 fl oz (⅞ cup)
ginger ale

1 fl oz (2 tablespoons)
lime juice

1 fl oz (2 tablespoons)
Simple Syrup
(see page 12)

10 mint leaves, plus
sprigs for garnish

lime slice,
for garnish

MOJITO

Muddle mint leaves in a cocktail shaker, add syrup, and lime juice along with ice, and shake. Top with ginger ale, then strain into a rocks glass filled with fresh ice. Garnish with a mint sprig and lime slice.

1½ fl oz (3 tablespoons)
lime juice

6 basil leaves,
plus more for garnish

4 cucumber slices,
plus more for garnish

1½ fl oz (3 tablespoons)
Simple Syrup (see page 12)

2 fl oz (¼ cup) water

CUCUMBER BASIL GIMLET

Preparation: 5 minutes
Serve in a rocks glass

Muddle basil leaves and cucumber in a cocktail shaker. Add lime juice, syrup, water, and ice and shake until chilled. Strain into a rocks glass filled with fresh ice and garnish with remaining basil and cucumber.

Celery Pink Salt (see page 20), for rim

2 fl oz (¼ cup) Simple Syrup
(see page 12)

2½ fl oz (⅓ cup)
lime juice

1 celery stalk, coarsely chopped,
plus leaves for garnish

1 fl oz (2 tablespoons)
orange juice

CELERY LIME-A-RITA

Preparation: 5 minutes
Serve in a margarita glass

Blend all the ingredients, except for the celery salt, in a blender until celery is
puréed. Strain, pressing out liquid from celery pulp. Pour liquid back into blender
and blend with ice, or shake liquid with ice in a cocktail shaker. Salt rim of glass
with celery salt, then pour in blended drink. Garnish with celery leaves.

1½ fl oz (3 tablespoons) lime juice

1½ fl oz (3 tablespoons) agave nectar

3 ripe cherry tomatoes, plus extra, halved, for garnish

very cold water, to top

Celery Pink Salt (see page 20), for rim

TOMATO COCKTAIL

Preparation: 5 minutes
Serve in a tall glass

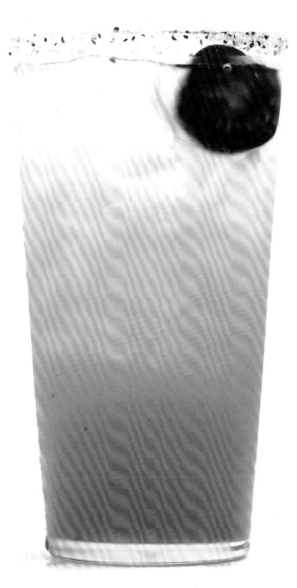

Muddle cherry tomatoes in a cocktail shaker, then add lime juice, agave nectar,
and ice and shake. Salt rim of tall glass with celery salt and add fresh ice.
Double strain into glass, top with water, and stir to combine.
Garnish with halved cherry tomato.

6 fl oz (¾ cup) milk

2 fl oz (¼ cup) lime juice

2 fl oz (¼ cup) sweetened
condensed milk

3 ears of corn, kernels removed

a pinch of saffron threads

lime slice, for garnish

SUN MILK

Preparation: 50 minutes
Serve in a tall or Collins glass

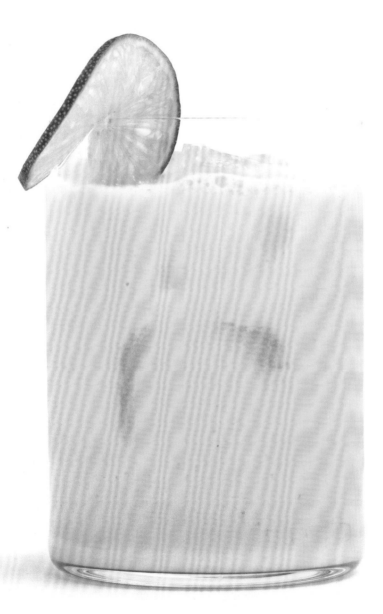

Purée corn kernels in a blender, then place in a small pan and simmer with milk for 30–45 minutes. Strain and let cool. Place mixture in a cocktail shaker with remaining ingredients, except for the lime slice, and ice. Shake until chilled. Double strain into a tall glass filled with fresh ice and garnish with lime.

8 fl oz (1 cup) water

3 borage leaves,
plus more for garnish

1 cup crushed ice

¾ fl oz (1½ tablespoons)
Simple Syrup (see page 12)

2 fl oz (¼ cup) lemon juice

BORAGE LEMONADE

Preparation: 5 minutes
Serve in a tall glass

Place all the ingredients in a blender and blend until borage is puréed.
Pour into a tall glass filled with fresh ice. Garnish with additional borage.

1½ fl oz (3 tablespoons)
Simple Syrup (see page 12)

½ lime, quartered (skin on)

2 tablespoons sweetened
condensed milk

3 fl oz (6 tablespoons) water

BRAZILIAN LIMEADE

Preparation: 5 minutes
Serve in a tall glass

Place lime quarters, condensed milk, syrup, and water in a blender and blend.
Strain through a fine sieve. Serve in a tall glass with a straw over ice.

2 fl oz (¼ cup) fresh turmeric juice
(Blend 1¼-inch piece of turmeric root with water
as needed in blender. Strain, pressing out juices.)

2 mint sprigs,
plus more for garnish

7 fl oz (⅞ cup)
young coconut water

1 lime wedge

COCONUT-TURMERIC REJUVENATOR

Preparation: 10 minutes
Serve in a tall glass

Muddle mint and lime wedge in a tall glass. Add turmeric juice, coconut water, and ice and stir together. Serve garnished with mint.

meyer lemon peel

2 fl oz (¼ cup) Meyer Lemon
Oleo Saccharum (see page 14)

2 strawberries, hulled and halved

4 fl oz (½ cup) meyer lemonade
or ordinary lemonade

½ cup crushed ice

WOODSY-BERRY LEMONADE

Preparation: 5 minutes
Serve in a tall glass

Combine all the ingredients, except for the meyer lemon peel, in a blender and blend until smooth. Pour into a tall glass and garnish with lemon peel.

1 fl oz (2 tablespoons) Herb-y
Blend Simple Syrup (see page 12)

4 fl oz (½ cup) peach juice

2 thin ripe peach
wedges, for garnish

tonic water, to top

¾ fl oz (1½ tablespoons)
lemon juice

¾ fl oz (1½ tablespoons)
pomegranate molasses

PEACHY KEEN

Preparation: 5 minutes
Serve in a rocks glass

Combine peach juice, syrup, lemon juice, and pomegranate molasses in a cocktail shaker with ice. Shake until chilled. Strain into a rocks glass filled with fresh ice, top with tonic water, and garnish with peaches inside glass.

8 fl oz (1 cup) soda water

16 fl oz (2 cups) açai juice

4 fl oz (½ cup)
orange juice

¼ lb sliced strawberries, ½ apple, diced,
and 1 small orange, sliced

4 fl oz (½ cup)
white grape juice

SANGRIA

Preparation: 5 minutes, plus 30 minutes chilling
Serve in a large pitcher with wine glasses

Combine all the ingredients, except for the soda water, in a large pitcher.
Leave in a refrigerator for 30 minutes. When ready to serve, add soda
water and pour into wine glasses filled with ice.

½ teaspoon vanilla extract

4 fl oz (½ cup) cashew milk
(any alternative milk or
regular dairy milk can
be substituted)

1 fl oz (2 tablespoons)
sweetened condensed milk

sparkling water,
to top

1 strawberry,
for garnish

2 fl oz (¼ cup)
Strawberry & Rhubarb
Shrub (see page 16)

STRAWBERRY RHUBARB PUNCH

Preparation: 5 minutes
Serve in a tall glass

Combine all the ingredients, except for the sparkling water and strawberry, in a cocktail shaker over ice and shake until chilled. Strain into a tall glass filled with fresh ice and top with sparkling water. Garnish with a strawberry.

tonic water, to top

6 fl oz (¾ cup)
unsweetened apricot juice

½ fl oz (1 tablespoon)
orange blossom water

2 fl oz (¼ cup) Herb-y Blend
Simple Syrup (see page 12)

1 mint sprig, for garnish

SUMMER APRICOT PUNCH

Preparation: 5 minutes
Serve in a rocks glass

Combine all the ingredients, except for the tonic water and mint, in a rocks glass and stir with ice. Top with tonic water and garnish with mint.

2 fl oz (¼ cup) lemonade

¾ fl oz (1½ tablespoons)
elderflower pressé

¾ fl oz (1½ tablespoons)
lime juice

2 mint sprigs,
plus more for garnish

lemon slices,
for garnish

ELDERFLOWER MINT LEMONADE

Preparation: 5 minutes
Serve in a tall glass

Muddle 2 mint sprigs at bottom of a tall glass. Add remaining ingredients,
except for the lemon slices and remaining mint, and ice and stir.
Garnish with lemon and remaining mint.

mint sprig and lime wedge,
for garnish

2 fl oz (¼ cup) lime juice

½ teaspoon molasses
or black treacle

8 fl oz (1 cup)
ginger beer

BRIGHT & SUNNY

Preparation: 5 minutes
Serve in a tall glass

Combine all the ingredients, except for the lime wedge and mint, in a tall glass
filled with crushed ice, layering molasses first, then ginger beer, and so on.
Garnish with lime wedge and mint.

2 teaspoons
granulated sugar

2 teaspoons cashew milk

2 teaspoons sweetened
condensed milk

½ teaspoon molasses or
blackstrap molasses

1 Thai black
tea bag

8 fl oz (1 cup) hot water

4 pieces dried mango,
plus additional dried mango,
cut into strips, for garnish

MANGO THAI ICED TEA

Preparation: 5 minutes, plus 10 minutes cooling
Serve in a tall or Collins glass

Steep tea bag, mangoes, sugar, and hot water in a large measuring cup or bowl
and let mixture cool. Remove mangoes and tea bag. Add remaining ingredients, stir.
Pour into a tall glass filled with ice and serve, garnished with mango strips.

2 fl oz (¼ cup) water

1 fl oz (2 tablespoons) lemon juice

4 fl oz (½ cup) cantaloupe purée
(cantaloupe whizzed in a blender)

½ fl oz (1 tablespoon) Lemon
Oleo Saccharum (see page 14)

2 thin melon wedges,
for garnish

SUMMER MELON COOLER

Preparation: 5 minutes
Serve in a rocks glass

Combine all the ingredients in a rocks glass and stir together.
Add ice and garnish with melon wedges.

2 mint sprigs, plus more for garnish

5 fl oz (10 tablespoons)
orange juice

5 fl oz (10 tablespoons) coconut milk

1½ oz dried banana

1 oz dried pineapple

2 pieces dried mango

pineapple wedge,
for garnish

TROPICAL FUSION

Preparation: 20 minutes
Serve in a tall glass

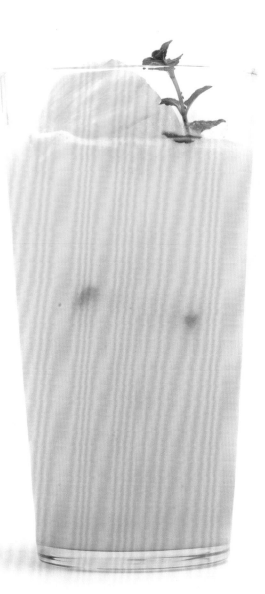

Bring all dried fruit and coconut milk to a boil in a pan. Reduce heat and simmer for 15 minutes until flavors infuse. Let cool, then place coconut mixture in a cocktail shaker with orange juice, mint, and ice and shake vigorously. Strain into a tall glass filled with fresh ice. Garnish with pineapple wedge and mint.

2 fl oz (¼ cup) orange juice

orange slice, for garnish

1 fl oz (2 tablespoons) Allspice Simple Syrup (see page 13)

4 fl oz (½ cup) cold brewed coffee

¾ fl oz (1½ tablespoons) milk

ICED COFFEE MOCKTAIL

Preparation: 5 minutes
Serve in a tall glass

Combine all the ingredients in a cocktail shaker with ice. Shake vigorously
until coffee and milk has become frothy. Pour contents into a tall glass
filled with fresh ice and garnish with orange slice.

1 fl oz (2 tablespoons) orange juice

orange twist, for garnish

1 fl oz (2 tablespoons)
white grape juice

4 fl oz (½ cup) Sanbitter

NOT YOUR NEGRONI

Preparation: 5 minutes
Serve in a rocks glass

Combine all the ingredients, except for the orange twist, in a mixing glass
and stir with ice until chilled. Strain into a rocks glass with fresh ice
and garnish with orange twist.

2 fl oz (¼ cup) lemon juice

1 fl oz (2 tablespoons)
Simple Syrup (see page 12)

1 cup crushed ice

¼ cup Roasted Pear Purée
(see page 18)

2 sage sprigs

PEAR SAGE SLUSHY

Preparation: 5 minutes
Serve in a rocks glass

Combine all the ingredients, except for 1 sage sprig, in a blender
and blend until smooth. Pour into a rocks glass and
garnish with the remaining sage sprig.

½ fl oz (1 tablespoon) Apple & Ginger Simple Syrup (see page 13)

½ fl oz (1 tablespoon) maple syrup

6 fl oz (¾ cup) nonalcoholic apple cider or apple juice

2 cinnamon sticks

MAPLE APPLE CIDER

Preparation: 20 minutes
Serve in a mug

Combine all the ingredients, except for the cinnamon sticks, in a small pan
and bring to a boil, then reduce heat and simmer for 15 minutes.
Serve hot in a mug, garnished with cinnamon sticks.

freshly grated nutmeg, for garnish

6 fl oz (¾ cup) ginger beer

⅜-inch piece of ginger,
plus a ginger slice for garnish

1 fl oz (2 tablespoons) Allspice
Simple Syrup (see page 13)

¼ cup Winter Squash Purée (see page 19)

FALL IN A CUP

Preparation: 5 minutes
Serve in a rocks glass

Place ginger in a mixing glass and muddle, then add purée and syrup.
Stir together until well combined. Add ginger beer and ice and stir.
Strain into a rocks glass over fresh ice and garnish with the
ginger slice and a light dusting of grated nutmeg.

2 fl oz (¼ cup) orange juice

8 fl oz (1 cup) water

2 tablespoons
granulated sugar

small piece of ginger, peeled
and thinly sliced

2 tablespoons tamarind pulp

orange slice, halved,
for garnish

TAMARIND GINGER

Preparation: 20 minutes
Serve in a rocks glass

Combine tamarind, water, ginger, and sugar in a small pan and simmer for 15 minutes. Let cool to room temperature, then strain into a cocktail shaker and add orange juice and ice. Shake vigorously, then pour into a rocks glass filled with fresh ice. Garnish with orange slice.

2 fl oz (¼ cup)
condensed milk

3 fl oz (6 tablespoons)
blood orange juice

soda water, to top

½ teaspoon
vanilla extract

¼ teaspoon orange flower water

blood orange slice,
for garnish

BLOOD ORANGE CREAMSICLE

Preparation: 5 minutes
Serve in a tall glass

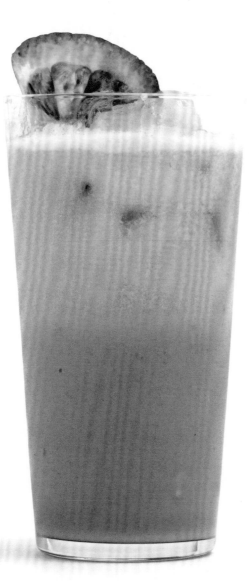

Combine all the ingredients, except for the soda water, in a cocktail shaker with ice and shake until chilled. Strain into a tall glass filled with fresh ice and top with soda water. Garnish with blood orange slice.

1 fl oz (2 tablespoons) lemon juice

1 fl oz (2 tablespoons) grapefruit juice

4 fl oz (½ cup)
Earl Grey tea, at
room temperature

2 fl oz (¼ cup)
Grapefruit Oleo Saccharum
(see page 15)

grapefruit peel twists,
for garnish

A BRIGHT SPOT ON A GRAY DAY

Preparation: 5 minutes
Serve in a stemmed glass

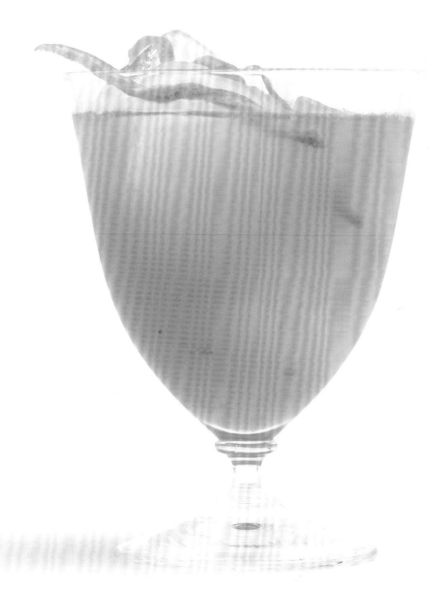

Combine all the ingredients in a cocktail shaker with ice and shake
until chilled. Strain into a stemmed glass filled with fresh ice and
garnish with grapefruit twists.

2 fl oz (¼ cup) milk

8 fl oz (1 cup) water

2 tablespoons granulated sugar
(depending on your sweetness level)

1 chai tea bag

½ ounce dried apple,
plus more for garnish

1 tablespoon
dried ginger

1-inch piece of
fresh turmeric root

cinnamon stick,
for garnish

TURMERIC, APPLE & GINGER CHAI

Preparation: 20 minutes
Serve in a mug or heatproof rocks glass

Place tea bag, water, apples, turmeric, and ginger in a small pan and bring
to a boil. Reduce heat, cover, and simmer for 15 minutes. Remove tea bag.
Add sugar and milk and whisk until sugar dissolves. Strain into a mug
or heatproof glass and garnish with cinnamon stick and dried apple.

sliced apple, for garnish

¼ cup Winter Squash Purée
(see page 19)

3 fl oz (6 tablespoons) Lapsang Souchong tea,
at room temperature

1 fl oz (2 tablespoons)
maple syrup

3 fl oz (6 tablespoons) nonalcoholic
apple cider or apple juice

SMOKY PUMPKIN

Preparation: 5 minutes
Serve in a rocks glass

Combine all the ingredients in a cocktail shaker and shake until chilled.
Strain into a rocks glass and garnish with an apple slice.

Plum slices,
for garnish

6 fl oz (¾ cup)
soda water

2 fl oz (¼ cup)
Plum & Cinnamon Shrub
(see page 16)

RED MOON

Preparation: 5 minutes
Serve in a rocks glass

Combine shrub and soda water in a rocks glass filled with ice and
stir until combined. Garnish with plum slices.

1½ fl oz (3 tablespoons)
ginger beer

4 fl oz (½ cup) carrot juice

2 fl oz (¼ cup)
orange juice

orange peel strips,
for garnish

WHAT'S UP, DOC?

Preparation: 6 minutes
Serve in a rocks glass

Combine all the ingredients in a rocks glass filled with ice and
stir together to combine. Garnish with orange peel strips.

6 fl oz (¾ cup) orange juice

orange peel strip,
for garnish

¼ cup Smoked Pineapple
Purée (see page 19)

1 fl oz (2 tablespoons)
macadamia nut milk

SMOKY ORANGE

Preparation: 5 minutes
Serve in a tall glass

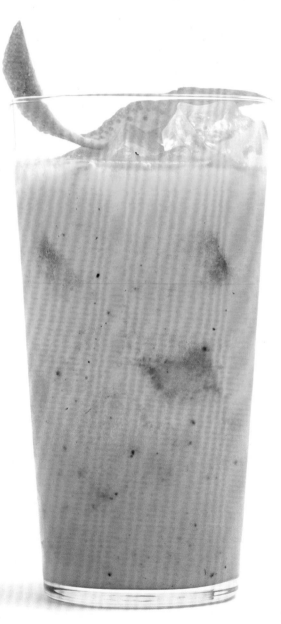

Combine all the ingredients in a cocktail shaker with ice
and shake until chilled. Strain into a tall glass filled with
fresh ice and serve with an orange peel twist.

2 fl oz (¼ cup) yuzu juice

1 fl oz (2 tablespoons)
elderflower syrup

soda water, to top

2 jalapeño chile slices, for garnish

4 fl oz (½ cup) yuzu tea,
at room temperature

Togarashi Salt
(see page 21), for rim

SPICY YUZU FIZZ

Preparation: 5 minutes
Serve in a tall or Collins glass

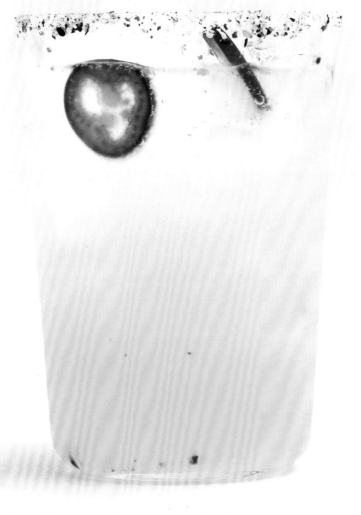

Combine all the ingredients, except for the soda water and salt,
with ice in a cocktail shaker and shake until chilled. Salt rim of a
tall or Collins glass. Strain drink into glass filled with fresh ice and
top with soda water. Garnish with chile slices.

2 fl oz (¼ cup) Allspice
Simple Syrup (see page 13)

4 fl oz (½ cup) nonalcoholic
apple cider or apple juice

2 fl oz (¼ cup) lemon juice

freshly grated nutmeg,
for garnish

2 tablespoons Winter
Squash Purée (see page 19)

1 egg white

SQUASH FLIP

Preparation: 5 minutes
Serve in a stemmed glass

Combine all the ingredients in a cocktail shaker without ice and
dry shake for 20–30 seconds until the egg white is emulsified.
Add ice to shaker and shake until chilled. Strain and serve in a
stemmed glass, garnished with grated nutmeg.

½ fl oz (1 tablespoon) lime juice

4 fl oz (½ cup) pineapple juice

½ fl oz (1 tablespoon) pomegranate juice

pineapple wedges
and cherry, for garnish

¼ cup Smoked Pineapple Purée
(see page 19)

SMOKY SINGAPORE SLING

Preparation: 5 minutes
Serve in a tall glass

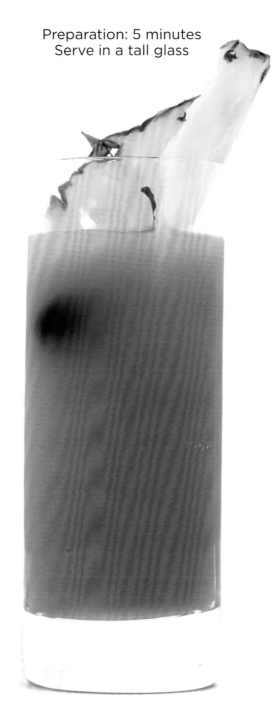

Combine all the ingredients in a cocktail shaker and shake until chilled.
Strain into a tall glass and garnish with pineapple wedges and a cherry.

ginger beer, to top

rosemary sprig,
for garnish

1 fl oz (2 tablespoons)
Kaffir Lime & Rosemary
Oleo-saccharum (see page 15)

2 fl oz (¼ cup)
lime juice

GINGER MULE

Preparation: 5 minutes
Serve in a tall glass

Stir all the ingredients, except for the ginger beer, in a tall glass over ice.
Stir well, top with ginger beer and stir once again until combined.
Garnish with a rosemary sprig.

freshly grated nutmeg,
for garnish

2 fl oz (¼ cup) whole milk

1 teaspoon vanilla extract

4 fl oz (½ cup) darjeeling tea,
at room temperature

2 fl oz (¼ cup) Allspice
Simple Syrup (see page 13)

WARMING MILK PUNCH

Preparation: 5 minutes
Serve in a mug or heatproof rocks glass

Warm all the ingredients in a small pan over low heat until hot.
Pour into a mug or heatproof glass and garnish with grated nutmeg.

2 fl oz (¼ cup) maple syrup

¼ oz dried orange

½ oz dried apple,
plus more for garnish

6 fl oz (¾ cup) nonalcoholic
apple cider or apple juice

1½ teaspoons
dried goji berries

4 whole cloves

2 cardamom pods

CARDAMOM-APPLE PIE

Preparation: 15 minutes
Serve in a mug or heatproof rocks glass

Combine all the ingredients in a small pan and simmer for 10 minutes until hot.
Once heated through and flavors have infused, strain and pour into a mug or
heatproof glass. Garnish with a dried apple slice.

8 fl oz (1 cup) dark roasted,
strong hot coffee (keep hot)

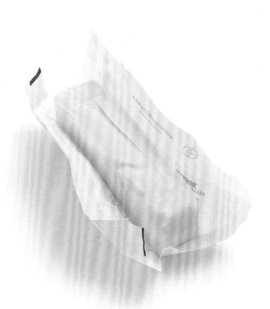

1 teaspoon unsalted butter

2 tablespoons
sweetened condensed milk

1 tablespoon coconut oil

COCONUT BULLET COFFEE

Preparation: 5 minutes
Serve in a mug or heatproof rocks glass

Place all the ingredients in a blender and whizz at high speed until frothy.
Pour into a mug or heatproof glass and serve.

4 fl oz (½ cup) Sanbitter

2 blood orange slices,
for garnish

1 fl oz (2 tablespoons) Grapefruit
Oleo Saccharum (see page 15)

1½ fl oz (3 tablespoons)
blood orange juice

BLOODY & BITTER

Preparation: 5 minutes
Serve in a tall or Collins glass

Place orange juice and oleo saccharum in a cocktail shaker and shake with ice. Add Sanbitter and stir to combine. Strain into a tall or Collins glass filled with fresh ice. Garnish with blood orange slices.

1 teaspoon ground turmeric

2 fl oz (¼ cup) lemon juice

2-inch piece of ginger,
peeled and finely grated

pinch of cayenne pepper,
plus more for garnish

4 fl oz (½ cup) orange juice

ORANGEADE

Preparation: 5 minutes
Serve in a rocks glass

Combine all the ingredients in a rocks glass filled with ice and stir until combined.
Add another pinch of cayenne pepper as a garnish.

1 fl oz (2 tablespoons) yuzu juice

1 tablespoon honey

soda water, to top

6 fl oz (¾ cup) Hoji Cha tea,
at room temperature

TOASTY YUZU

Preparation: 5 minutes
Serve in a stemmed glass

Combine all the ingredients, except soda water, in a cocktail shaker
and shake until chilled. Strain and pour into a stemmed glass filled
with fresh ice, then top with soda water.

handful of conifer needles (can be substituted with white pine, spruce, or douglas fir)

½ fl oz (1 tablespoon) maple syrup

8 fl oz (1 cup) cashew milk

freshly grated nutmeg, for garnish

PINING AWAY

Preparation: 35 minutes
Serve in a rocks glass

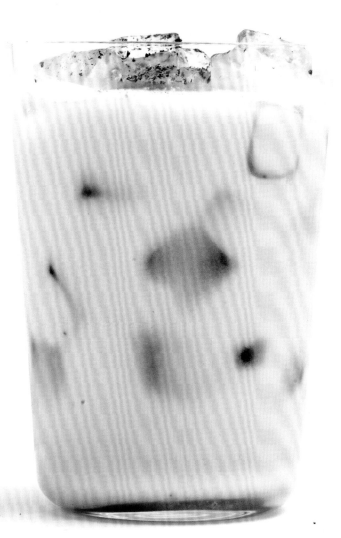

Combine conifer needles and cashew milk in a small pan over medium-high heat
and simmer for 30 minutes, or until flavors are infused. Let cool. Place cooled
liquid and maple syrup in a cocktail shaker with ice and shake until chilled.
Strain into a rocks glass filled with fresh ice and garnish with grated nutmeg.

For the batter:

¾ cup granulated sugar

¾ cup brown sugar

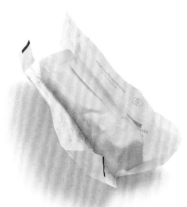

½ cup butter,
at room temperature

1 teaspoon
ground cinnamon

¼ teaspoon
ground cloves

¼ teaspoon
ground nutmeg

1½ cups vanilla (or
gingersnap) ice cream,
slightly softened

For the hot buttered yum:

boiling water

cinnamon stick and star anise,
for garnish

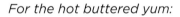

HOT BUTTERED YUM

Preparation: 5 minutes
Serve in mugs or heatproof rocks glasses

To make the batter, mix butter, sugars, and spices thoroughly in a bowl. Stir in ice cream and mix until well combined. Transfer batter to a container with a tight-fitting lid and store in the freezer for up to 2 weeks. To serve the hot buttered yum, place a portion of the batter in a mug or heatproof glass, fill with boiling water, and stir. Garnish with a cinnamon stick and star anise.

6 fl oz (¾ cup) milk

1 egg, whisked

½ teaspoon ground cinnamon,
plus more for garnish

¾ fl oz (1½ tablespoons)
maple syrup

¼ cup Spiced Persimmon Purée
(see page 18)

PERSIMMON NOG

Preparation: 10 minutes
Serve in a mug or heatproof rocks glass

Warm milk in a small pan over low heat and add egg slowly while whisking
to make sure it doesn't cook in milk mixture. Heat until warm but not too hot
and take off heat. Add remaining ingredients and stir to mix well. Garnish with
a sprinkle of ground cinnamon on top.

soda water, to top

1 fl oz (2 tablespoons)
lemon juice

2 fl oz (¼ cup)
grapefruit juice

1 fl oz (2 tablespoons)
Simple Syrup
(see page 12)

sea salt, for rim

grapefruit slice,
for garnish

PALOMA

Preparation: 5 minutes
Serve in a Champagne glass

Salt rim of Champagne glass with sea salt. Combine all the ingredients,
except for the grapefruit slice, in glass filled with ice and mix well.
Serve, garnished with grapefruit slice.

orange slices, for garnish

6 fl oz (¾ cup) water

sage, for garnish

2 fl oz (¼ cup) Cranberry & Sage
Shrub (see page 17)

3 fl oz (6 tablespoons)
meyer lemon juice

MEYER LEMON CRANBERRY

Preparation: 5 minutes
Serve in a tall glass

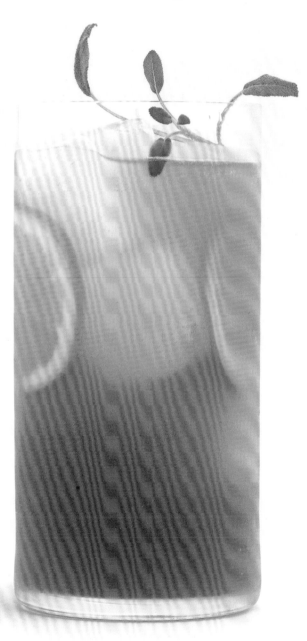

Combine all the ingredients in a cocktail shaker with ice and shake until chilled.
Pour into a tall glass filled with fresh ice. Rub a sage leaf in your hands to release
the oils and place on top of drink as a garnish along with orange slices.

4 fl oz (½ cup) macadamia nut milk

orange peel strips, for garnish

2 mint sprigs

1 tablespoon kumquat
or orange marmalade

2 fl oz (¼ cup) orange juice

MINTY ORANGE & MACADAMIA PUNCH

Preparation: 5 minutes
Serve in a rocks glass

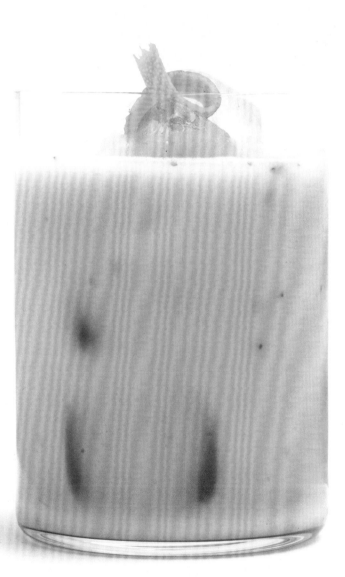

Muddle mint in the bottom of a cocktail shaker. Add the remaining ingredients
with ice and shake until chilled. Strain into a rocks glass filled with fresh ice
and garnish with orange peel strips.

8 fl oz (1 cup) Lapsang Souchong tea, hot

1 tablespoon honey

lemon wedge, for garnish

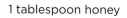

2 fl oz (¼ cup) lemon juice

HOT TODDY

Preparation: 5 minutes
Serve in a mug or heatproof rocks glass

Combine all the ingredients in a mug or heatproof glass.
Serve, garnished with lemon wedge.

2 fl oz (¼ cup) kaffir lime
(or ordinary lime) juice

2 fl oz (¼ cup) lemonade

2 fl oz (¼ cup) Kaffir Lime &
Rosemary Oleo-saccharum
(see page 15)

1 egg white

rosemary sprig, for garnish

KAFFIR LIME & ROSEMARY FLIP

Preparation: 5 minutes
Serve in a stemmed glass

Combine all the ingredients in a cocktail shaker without ice and dry shake for
20–30 seconds until the egg white is emulsified. Add ice and shake until chilled.
Strain and serve in a stemmed glass with no ice, garnished with rosemary.

6 fl oz (¾ cup) nonalcoholic
apple cider or apple juice

1 tablespoon
pomegranate molasses

4 whole cloves

1 cardamom pod

2 star anise pods

1 cinnamon stick

POMEGRANATE APPLE SPICED CIDER

Preparation: 15 minutes
Serve in a mug or heatproof rocks glass

Combine apple cider and spices in a small pan and bring to a boil. Reduce heat
and simmer for 10 minutes until spices are infused. Add pomegranate molasses
and stir to combine. Serve in a mug or heatproof glass.

28 fl oz (3½ cups) water

½ cup granulated sugar

1 tablespoon allspice berries

1 tablespoon hibiscus flowers,
plus more for garnish

4 thin slices
of ginger

1 cinnamon stick

lime slices, for garnish

WINTER SPICED HIBISCUS

Preparation: 10 minutes, plus 30 minutes standing
Serve in a pitcher and tall glasses

Combine sugar, 14 fl oz (1¾ cups) of the water, allspice berries, ginger, and cinnamon in a small pan and bring to a boil. Stir until sugar has dissolved. Remove from heat and stir in hibiscus flowers, then cover and let sit for 30 minutes. Strain and pour into a large pitcher, add ice and remaining water. Pour into tall glasses filled with fresh ice and garnish with lime slices and hibiscus flowers.

1 cinnamon stick

1–2 tablespoons brown sugar (depending on how sweet you want it to be)

7 fl oz (⅞ cup) water

2 pieces dried persimmon

½-inch piece of ginger

PERSIMMON CINNAMON TEA

Preparation: 15 minutes
Serve in a mug or heatproof rocks glass

In a small pan, combine 1 piece dried persimmon with the remaining ingredients, except for the cinnamon stick, and bring to a boil. Reduce heat, cover, and simmer for 10 minutes. Pour into a mug or heatproof glass and serve with remaining piece of dried persimmon and the cinnamon stick.

8 fl oz (1 cup) toasted buckwheat tea,
made with 2 tablespoons toasted buckwheat
and 8 fl oz (1 cup) hot water

½-inch piece of ginger

1 fl oz (2 tablespoons)
maple syrup

1 fl oz (2 tablespoons)
rice vinegar

TOAST TEA

Preparation: 20 minutes
Serve in a mug or heatproof rocks glass

Combine buckwheat tea, maple syrup, and ginger in a small pan and
simmer for 15 minutes. Remove from heat and add vinegar.
Pour into a mug or heatproof glass and serve.

16 fl oz (2 cups) cranberry juice

6 fl oz (¾ cup) orange juice

3 fl oz (6 tablespoons)
Cranberry & Sage Shrub
(see page 17)

4 pieces dried orange

orange slices and
cranberries, for garnish

1 tablespoon juniper berries,
lightly crushed

WINTER PUNCH

Preparation: 10 minutes
Serve in a large pitcher with rocks glasses

Combine shrub, dried oranges, and juniper berries in a small pan
and simmer for 5 minutes until flavors are combined. Let cool. Combine
both juices and shrub mixture in a large pitcher with ice and stir well.
Pour into rocks glasses and garnish with orange slices and cranberries.

4 fl oz (½ cup) blood orange juice

Wild Fennel Sugar
(see page 21), for rim

1 fl oz (2 tablespoons) ginger syrup
(Blend one or two 3-inch pieces of sliced
ginger with water as needed in blender.
Strain, pressing out juices.)

2 fl oz (¼ cup) lime juice

BLOOD ORANGE GINGER-A-RITA

Preparation: 5 minutes
Serve in a Champagne glass

Combine all the ingredients, except fennel sugar, in a blender with
ice and blend until smooth. Sugar rim of a Champagne glass
with fennel sugar. Pour blended drink into glass and serve.

1½ tablespoons
dried lemongrass

½ oz dried meyer lemon

8 fl oz (1 cup) hot water

1–2 mint sprigs, for garnish

1 fl oz (2 tablespoons)
Meyer Lemon Oleo Saccharum
(see page 14)

lemon slices, for garnish

WINTER GRASS

Preparation: 5 minutes, plus 2 minutes standing
Serve in a mug or heatproof rocks glass

Combine all the ingredients, except oleo-saccharum, mint, and lemon slices, in a heatproof pitcher and steep for 2 minutes. Strain into a mug or heatproof glass and stir in oleo saccharum. Garnish with mint and lemon slices.

4 fl oz (½ cup) grapefruit juice

lemon-lime soda, to top

2 fl oz (¼ cup) Grapefruit
Oleo Saccharum
(see page 15)

Chile Black Salt
(see page 20), for rim

grapefruit slice, for garnish

SALTY DOG

Preparation: 5 minutes
Serve in a Champagne glass

Salt rim of a Champagne glass with Chile Black Salt. Combine juice and oleo saccharum in glass over ice and stir well. Top with soda and garnish with grapefruit slice.

3 whole cloves

2 fl oz (¼ cup) pomegranate juice

6 fl oz (¾ cup) blackcurrant juice

cinnamon stick,
for garnish

2 blackberries

½ oz dried orange,
plus more for garnish

MULLED WINTER PUNCH

Preparation: 20 minutes
Serve in a mug or heatproof rocks glass

Combine all the ingredients, except for cinnamon stick and dried orange slices,
in a small pan and bring to a boil. Reduce heat and simmer for 10–15 minutes.
Strain into a mug or heatproof glass and garnish with cinnamon stick
and dried orange slices.

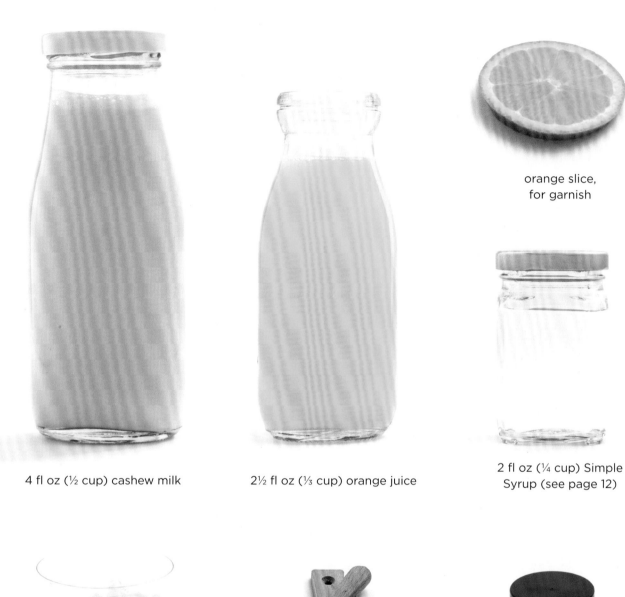

4 fl oz (½ cup) cashew milk

2½ fl oz (⅓ cup) orange juice

orange slice, for garnish

2 fl oz (¼ cup) Simple Syrup (see page 12)

½ cup crushed ice

½ banana

1 teaspoon vanilla extract

ORANGE YOU GLAD TO SEE ME

Preparation: 5 minutes
Serve in a tall or Collins glass

Combine all the ingredients, except for the orange slice, in a blender
and blend until smooth. Pour into a tall or Collins glass and
garnish with an orange slice.

INDEX

INDEX

Publisher: Catie Ziller

Author: Caroline Hwang

Photographer: Beatriz da Costa

Food stylists: Cyd McDowell & Frances Boswell

Designer & illustrator: Alice Chadwick

Editor: Kathy Steer

Published in the United States by Weldon Owen,
a division of Insight Editions.

Library of Congress Cataloging-in-Publication data is available

ISBN: 978-1-68188-435-6

Printed and bound in China.

This edition printed in 2021

10 9 8 7 6 5 4 3